On War, Food, and Gods: Culinary Tales of Resilience in Times of Conflict

Ginger L Franklin, PhD.

In the bread we break,

God whispers of peace,

where war divides,

meals unite—equal in hunger,

shared in hope.

Introduction

In a world where conflict often takes center stage, shaping the contours of history and human experience, there lies an intricate, often overlooked narrative – the story of food. "On War, Food, and Gods" digs into this uncharted terrain, exploring the profound relationship between food and humanity through the lens of war, conflict, and religious diversity.

This collection of short stories, drawn from personal encounters and firsthand accounts, serves as a testament to the power of the human spirit and the pivotal role food plays in our lives, especially during times of turmoil. Though I have changed some of the names in the stories, all of the events are true. I've been collecting these stories for over a decade, and I am happy to finally be sharing them with you in this work.

Food, in its essence, is more than just sustenance. It is an intimate dish spiced with cultural identity, tradition, and memory. Amidst the ravages of war and the divides of religious conflict, food emerges as a silent narrator, capturing the adaptability and power of people.

Each story in this collection is a window into how food becomes a symbol of resistance, a comfort during adversity, and a tool for survival.

But why tell these stories? Beyond their narrative appeal, they serve a dual purpose. Firstly, they act as a bridge connecting us to the diverse experiences of others, fostering empathy and understanding in a world often marred by differences. Secondly, these tales serve an educational purpose, bringing to light the nuanced ways in which food trends and cultures evolve under the pressures of war and conflict.

The study of food in the context of conflict and religion is rich and multifaceted. Anthropologists and sociologists have long pointed out how food habits and preferences are deeply influenced by societal changes, especially during periods of strife. Conflict not only disrupts food systems and availability but also influences food practices and rituals.

For example, scarcity during wartime can lead to innovation in the kitchen, birthing new recipes and ways of cooking. Similarly, religious restrictions and observances play a significant role in shaping dietary habits, influencing everything from agricultural practices to culinary traditions.

In this collection, the framework provided by Claude Lévi-Strauss's culinary triangle becomes a vital lens through which we can view food as a form of language that communicates cultural values, particularly in times of war and conflict. Lévi-Strauss proposed that how a culture prepares and consumes food – be it raw, cooked, or spoiled – is a method of expressing its identity and worldview.

As readers journey through the stories, they will see how families and communities in warzones adapt their culinary practices, subtly narrating their tales of resilience, cultural preservation, and adaptation in the face of adversity. The way a dish is prepared or modified in response to changing circumstances becomes a silent yet profound declaration of enduring cultural values and a testament to the human spirit's versatility.

Similarly, Arjun Appadurai's insights into the relationship between cuisine, culture, and political identity offer a compelling angle for exploring these narratives. Appadurai's perspective can be applied to understanding how food becomes more than sustenance in these stories; it is a symbol of communal identity, a point of contention or unity, reflecting the socio-political and religious fabric of each setting.

For instance, in the story set in Old Delhi, the differing dietary practices of Hindu and Muslim communities transcend mere personal preference, revealing deep-rooted cultural and religious identities. These culinary choices become intertwined with the larger narrative of communal harmony and discord, illustrating how food practices are inextricably linked to the socio-political narratives of communities.

As we explore these stories, these theoretical frameworks invite us to not only engage with the narratives on a human level but also to appreciate the profound sociocultural underpinnings of culinary practices.

This collection, therefore, is not just an anthology of stories from conflict zones; it is an exploration of how food – in all its forms and meanings – becomes a powerful instrument in understanding and narrating the human experience in times of turmoil.

Each story in this compilation, be it set in the pomegranate fields of Afghanistan, the bustling lanes of Old Delhi, or among the ruins of a war-torn land, offers a unique perspective on the human condition. They are not just tales of survival but are imbued with the flavors of hope, strength, and the unyielding human spirit.

In "On War, Food, and Gods," you will find more than stories. You will discover a world where food transcends its physical form to become a symbol of perseverance, a beacon of cultural heritage, and a bridge connecting people as well as the past, present, and future.

Through these narratives, I aim to offer not just insight into diverse human experiences but also to underscore the incredible power of food as a cultural and emotional anchor in times of turmoil.

As you embark on this journey through the pages, it is my hope that these stories resonate with you, offering both enlightenment and a deeper appreciation for the complex dish that is our shared human experience.

A Harvest of Courage

In the heart of a small Ukrainian village, nestled between the whispering pines and rolling hills, war had left an ugly scar. It was not just the physical mark of mines hidden like treacherous seeds in the soil, but a deeper, more painful wound in the hearts of its residents. The village, once a place of life and laughter, now lay under the shadow of fear and scarcity.

As the war dragged on, the villagers faced a dire situation. The once-reliable supply of food had dwindled to a trickle, the roads cut off, the fields too dangerous to harvest. Despair crept into their homes like an unwelcome ghost, whispering of hunger and hopelessness.

It was in these desperate times that the village elders gathered to discuss their situation with others in the village. Together, the elders were a portrait of grace, wisdom etched into their faces like the lines of an ancient map. Among them was Olena, her silver hair as luminous as the moon, and Yora, whose eyes held the quiet strength of the forest. They remembered the days when the village was young, when they ran through the woods, foraging for mushrooms and herbs.

"These woods are our ancestors' legacy." Olena said, her voice steady. "They have fed us before, and they can feed us again."

"But the mines?" A younger villager argued, his voice laced with fear. "It's a death walk."

"We know these woods." Petro replied, his voice resonating with a certainty that silenced all doubts. "We have been walking these paths since we were children, and later, as young lovers, and as parents. The forest is in our blood."

And so, with the strength that only comes with age and experience, the elders devised a plan. They drew upon the collective memory of their youth, recalling the safest paths, the hidden trails, the secret clearings.

They shared stories, each one a piece of the puzzle, a guide through the treacherous terrain. They would know where the mines were just as one might notice a new blemish on their cheek.

Early the next morning, as the sun cast a golden glow over the village, the elders set out. They moved with a cautious grace, their steps light, their senses attuned to the whispers of the trees and vegetation in the woods. They knew the risks, but the thought of their children, their grandchildren, going hungry was a greater fear than any mine could instill.

The villagers watched, their hearts a mix of fear and awe, as the elders disappeared into the embrace of the branches and shadows. They waited, each minute stretching into an eternity, each sound a potential harbinger of tragedy or hope.

Hours passed, and just as the sun began to dip below the horizon, painting the sky in hues of fire and gold, the elders returned. Their baskets were heavy with wild mushrooms and herbs.

The village erupted in joy, tears mixing with laughter, as the elders distributed their precious cargo. The bounty of the forest was laid out like a feast of survival. That night, as the elders and a few other villagers gathered around a roaring fire, the aroma of mushroom stew filling the air, there was a sense of unity, of triumph, even in the darkest of times.

"The forest has provided," Olena said, her eyes reflecting the flames. "And so have we." She then sat in silence reflecting on her youth and how things had changed, and yet…had not.

In that moment, the elders were not just the aged of the village; they were its guardians, its heart, its hope. They had faced the remnants of war, the specter of starvation, and had emerged victorious. Their courage, their love for their village, was a beacon of light in a world shadowed by conflict.

And as the stars came out, twinkling like brighter memories in the night sky, the village found comfort in the thought that even in the midst of war's unfair desolation, there was still hope, still life, and most importantly, there was still a community standing strong together.

*****

The conflict in Ukraine, especially since its escalation in 2022, profoundly affected everyday life for millions. When Russia intensified its military campaign, a full-scale war, it wasn't just about territorial control; it deeply impacted the Ukrainian people and the democratic world overall.

Families, once living peaceful lives, suddenly found themselves in the midst of a rapidly unfolding crisis. The invasion led to widespread displacement, with many having to leave behind homes, livelihoods, and memories. The countryside, towns, and cities faced significant turmoil, drastically altering the social fabric and sense of security that people once knew.

In the midst of this, the perseverance of the Ukrainian people became prominently visible. Faced with uncertainty and danger, communities banded together, finding strength in unity. Despite the overwhelming challenges, including the fear of violence and the struggle to access basic necessities, their spirit of perseverance shone through.

This resilience wasn't just in resisting the military invasion but also in adapting to a rapidly changed way of life, finding ways to support each other in times of dire need. The conflict, while bringing undeniable hardship, also highlighted the enduring strength and solidarity of the Ukrainian people in the face of adversity.

Culturing Time

In the sprawling evacuee camp set against the backdrop of El Paso's arid landscape, a rhythm of life slowly emerged amidst the canvas of temporary tent housing and the constant murmur of hopeful yet weary and worried voices. Among these voices was that of an Afghan evacuee, fondly referred to as "the Professor" by the camp staff and interpreters.

The Professor, a dignified man with a scholarly appearance, had become a familiar figure at the camp. Each day, like clockwork, he approached the same desk inside of the same tent, always with the same pressing question: "When can we leave?" His inquiries were met with sympathetic smiles and words of assurance, but no definite answers.

As weeks turned into months at the camp, a surprising revelation came to light. The Professor's daily visits were not driven solely by his eagerness to leave the El Paso tent city; they were an escape from the relentless haranguing of his daughter, who, trapped in the misery of camp life, found her frustrations uncontainable.

Daily, the daughter would harass her father for answers. When would they leave? Where were they going? Nobody knew, but the Professor felt an obligation to at least ask for some answers.

Gradually, the Professor's routine was transformed. What began as inquiries about departure evolved into leisurely chats with the interpreters and staff. He spoke of Afghanistan, of his life before the chaos, and he also listened intently to the stories of those around him.

These conversations became a refuge, a brief respite from the uncertainty that enveloped them all. And certainly, his daughter could feel slightly more at ease knowing that her father had been out all day collecting intel, such as it was.

Then, one day, the Professor brought something unexpected into the main information tent: homemade yogurt. The staff, now his friends, were initially wary of the delicacy prepared under such rudimentary conditions. How did he make yogurt in his tent?

They looked at each other with suspicion, yet all tried some of the yogurt. Nobody got sick and it tasted quite nice! They were all soon won over by its creamy texture and tangy taste. Each day, they looked forward to this simple yet heartfelt gesture, wondering how he managed such a feat in a desert camp.

The Professor, it turned out, had a knack for resourcefulness. With limited supplies and sheer ingenuity, he had fashioned a makeshift yogurt incubator, using the warmth of the El Paso sun and the little milk that he had.

The yogurt wasn't just a treat; it was a testament to his ability to find joy and a gift of thanks and friendship for the staff who had welcomed his daily queries.

As the days passed, the yogurt became more than just something to eat; it became a symbol of shared experiences and community that can be found even in hardship. The Professor would bring his yogurt and the staff would make him a cup of tea and offer Oreos.

They would sit at the old military desk under the tent roof and chat for hours snacking and drinking tea. This scene was a reminder that life, with all its flavors, continued to churn, even in an evacuee camp full of heartbreak and anxiety.

Then, unexpectedly, the day came. The staff, with a mix of happiness and sorrow, informed the Professor that he and his daughter were to be relocated to Virginia. There was a sense of finality in that announcement, a closing of a chapter that had been written together in the desert sands.

The Professor left the camp, taking with him the memories and stories shared. The staff, left behind, found themselves missing the daily ritual, the comforting presence of the Professor, and, of course, the yogurt that had unexpectedly become a part of their lives.

The staff at the old military desk bought the Professor and his daughter a set of luggage. In a final exchange, they gave him the suitcases which were filled with supplies and Oreos, and he gave them each a final serving of yogurt and a warm hug. They never saw the Professor again, but his legacy lingered in those fleeting moments of connection and the unforgettable taste of yogurt made under the El Paso sun.

In August of 2021, the evacuation from Afghanistan became a defining moment in the country's history, illustrating both the complexities of international conflicts and the human cost of abrupt transitions in power. The rapid advancement of the Taliban across Afghanistan, following the withdrawal of international forces, led to a chaotic and traumatic evacuation process resulting in deaths, displacement, and general devastation.

Thousands of Afghans, fearing for their lives and the safety of their families due to their work aiding the U.S. military, rushed to leave the country. This mass exodus was marked by scenes of desperation and chaos, particularly at Kabul airport, where people thronged in a frantic bid to secure a spot on the few evacuation flights.

The aftermath of the evacuation saw the establishment of evacuee camps, primarily on U.S. military bases, under Operation Allies Welcome. These camps became temporary homes for thousands of Afghan evacuees, offering a semblance of safety but also symbolizing the upheaval they had endured and the impermanence of safety. Life in these camps, while structured to provide basic necessities and some level of security, was a far cry from the lives the evacuees had left behind.

Evacuees faced the trauma of abrupt displacement, the anxiety of an uncertain future, and the challenge of adapting to a completely new environment. The camps served as transitional spaces where evacuees received medical screenings, vaccinations, and initial processing (vetting) before being resettled into various communities across the United States.

For many, these camps were the first step in a long journey of rebuilding their lives in unfamiliar surroundings, far from the homes they had been forced to flee.

I worked at Fort Bliss evacuee camp from August 29th until it closed on December 30th. There, we in-processed and resettled over 11,000 Afghan evacuees. It was the second largest evacuee camp in the U.S. I hope one day, I can again cross paths with the Professor, my favorite guest.

Halal and Ahimsa

In the narrow, labyrinthine lanes of Old Delhi, an area steeped in history and simmering with cultural tensions, lived two boys – Arjun, a Hindu, and Irfan, a Muslim. Their friendship, a picture of perfect innocence, blossomed in the shadows of a city that bore the scars of past conflicts and the strain of present disagreements.

Old Delhi, a microcosm of India's vast diversity, had witnessed the brutal aftermath of the Partition in 1947, a seismic event that uprooted millions and sowed deep seeds of mistrust between Hindu and Muslim communities. The horrors of that time, though decades past, lingered in the collective memory, occasionally resurfacing in moments of tension.

The boys, however, remained untouched by this history until an event fractured the fragile peace in their neighborhood. The issue arose from the very essence of daily life – food. In the dense fabric of Old Delhi, culinary practices were not just a matter of taste but a declaration of identity and deep religious traditions.

Irfan's family, adhering to Islamic halal methods of butchery, unknowingly sparked discomfort among their Hindu neighbors. The sight of meat being prepared, with streams of blood occasionally spilling onto the streets, conflicted with the Hindu principle of Ahimsa, the practice of non-violence and vegetarianism.

As whispers turned to murmurs and murmurs into shouts, the neighborhood's coexistence began to fray. The aunties and uncles, once amicable, were now hearing echoes of a divided past.

Arjun's parents saw the butchery as an aggressive dismissal of their beliefs, a reminder of the violent division of their nation. Irfan's family felt their practices, a fundamental part of their faith, were under siege, reminiscent of past oppressions.

Caught in this crossfire, Arjun and Irfan's friendship became a silent casualty. The boys, who once played together without care, now walked with the weight of their families' histories and the bitterness of their community.

They met less frequently; their conversations strained under the heavy gaze of their respective communities.

In a twist of fate, echoing the dark chapters of history, the tension in the neighborhood escalated. A minor altercation between members of the two communities spiraled out of control, leading to a night of chaos that mirrored the terrible communal riots that had periodically plagued Delhi.

The streets of Old Delhi, which had seen centuries of history, now witnessed the resurgence of an old wound. Streams of blood in the streets, be it animal or human, were as impotent offerings to gods who refused to intervene.

In the aftermath, Arjun and Irfan found themselves on opposite sides of a barricade, their friendship lost in the smoke and cries of a divided neighborhood. The realization that their bond could not withstand the tidal wave of historical animosity was a silent tragedy in itself.

The riot faded, but its scars remained, both in the physical space of the neighborhood and in the hearts of its residents.

Arjun and Irfan, now under the mere shadows of a shared past, moved on with their lives, carrying the weight of a lesson learned too early – that the weight of history can bring down even the purest of friendships.

In this tale, there was no reconciliation, and no shared meals to bridge the divide.

Instead, there was only the lingering sense of what could have been, a friendship that could have challenged history but instead became another casualty of its unyielding march.

*****

The Partition of India in 1947, a pivotal moment in South Asian history, led to the creation of two independent nations, India and Pakistan. This event was a direct outcome of the Indian Independence Act passed by the British Parliament, marking the end of British colonial rule in the region.

The division was primarily based on religious demographics, with majority-Muslim areas forming Pakistan and majority-Hindu areas constituting India. The partition resulted in one of the largest and most brutal migrations in modern history, as approximately 14-18 million people crossed the newly drawn borders, with Hindus and Sikhs moving to India, and Muslims to Pakistan.

The process of the partition was hasty and traumatic, characterized by little warning and a lack of proper planning. This abruptness and the deep-seated religious tensions led to widespread and horrific violence, resulting in the deaths of up to two million people.

The landscape bore witness to unspeakable atrocities, including trains full of corpses, widespread rape, and pillaging on all sides. Sikhs, Hindus, and Muslims were all driven to desperation and terror because of the partition.

Communities that had coexisted for centuries suddenly found themselves embroiled in devastating conflict, fueled by hastily drawn borders, rising nationalist rhetoric, and the divisive policies of the British colonial administration.

The impact of the Partition of India resonates to this day, shaping the national consciousness and the relationship between India, Pakistan, and later Bangladesh. It serves as a sobering reminder of the fragility of peace and the potential for deep divides within societies.

Adila's Forbidden Fruit

In the heart of Afghanistan's pomegranate fields, where the earth sang with the colors of the harvest, there lived a girl named Adila. Her home was nestled among ancient groves where pomegranate trees, stoic and enduring, spread their boughs like protective arms over the lands and inhabitants. Adila's days were painted with the hues of these fruits – a deep, life-affirming red that mirrored the laughter and dreams of a girl on the cusp of blooming into adulthood.

As the pomegranates ripened, their skins splitting to reveal the jeweled seeds within, Adila's world too was ripening, full of possibilities and sweet promises. The pomegranate, with its myriad of seeds, was a symbol of the abundant opportunities she saw growing before her.

Each day, after helping in the orchards, she hurried to school, her mind as thirsty for knowledge as the parched earth for rain. Often, she would bring the best pomegranate from the morning harvesting and place it on her teacher's desk before class started. She thought her teacher didn't know who placed the delicious gift, but Adila was the only girl in class who came to school with red stains on her hands.

But in 2021, the winds of her world shifted, blowing in a storm that had long been brewing in the distance. The Taliban reclaimed their hold on Afghanistan, their shadow falling ominously over the valleys and the lives thriving within, especially the lives of women and girls. The decree came swiftly and irrevocably – girls were no longer permitted to attend school. The gates of learning, which had stood open for Adila, clanged shut, severing her from her dreams.

The change was as noticeable and disheartening as the dryness that crept into the soil of the pomegranate orchards. Unable to work, sell the pomegranates at the market, or take proper care the trees, the women and girls in Adila's family stayed indoors and fell into a hopeless despair.

The trees, once lush and vibrant, began to wilt, their leaves curling, their fruits dwindling. The red of the pomegranates, once a symbol of life and prosperity, seemed to weep for the dreams now buried beneath the oppressive regime. Everything in Adila's life seemed to take on a hue of brown and grey.

Adila watched, her heart sinking, as her world contracted. The school stood silent, a haunting reminder of what had been snatched away. She would wander the orchards, running her fingers over the withering fruits, their once-vibrant red now a dull echo of her own subdued spirit.

In the confines of her home, she held a pomegranate in her hands, its seeds no longer symbols of hope but of a fractured future. The deep red, reminiscent of the vitality and spirit of womanhood, now whispered tales of loss, of freedoms bled away, of a life constrained.

Yet in the hush of dawn, when the first light kissed the tops of the pomegranate trees, Adila's resolve stirred. She clung to her dreams with a quiet defiance, believing in a future where the orchards would once again flourish, where the gates of learning would reopen for her and for all the girls like her.

In the secret spaces of her heart, she nurtured her aspirations, much like the hidden seeds of the pomegranate, waiting for the day they could burst forth into the world, vibrant and unyielding.

For in Adila's dreams lay the promise of a time when the pomegranate orchards would once again be a symbol of life and vibrancy that she could share with her teacher.

Since the Taliban's takeover of Afghanistan in August 2021, their policies and practices have significantly impacted the rights and freedoms of women and girls in the country. The Taliban have implemented various measures that severely restrict women's participation in public life.

Women have been excluded from political roles and most jobs in the public sector, and their access to education beyond primary school has been prohibited. This ban on education significantly limits their professional opportunities and personal development.

The Taliban's approach to women's rights has been met with widespread international condemnation. Despite this, they have continued their restrictive policies. The closure of beauty salons, for example, not only impacted the livelihood of millions of women but also signified the loss of one of the few women-only spaces outside the home.

The Taliban have also targeted women working in aid agencies, exacerbating the crisis for women and girls who depend on these services. Women who protest these policies face severe consequences, including arbitrary detention, enforced disappearance, and torture.

In recent news, as of 2024, Taliban leaders have announced that women who are accused of adultery can be stoned to death. Women are not allowed to leave their home without the accompaniment of a male blood relative, and even then, it is rare for them to go outside of the home.

The Green Wave

2023 - Jass sat in the back of her Uber heading to Bangkok's largest outdoor shopping area, Chatuchak Weekend Market. She passively watched as scooter after scooter, each donning the trademark green Grab livery sped, crept, or lane split their way to the front of each street, gathering in groups in front of the four-wheeled traffic to wait for the red lights to turn green. She turned to her husband and suggested they try Grab delivery for dinner sometime during their stay in the city. Little did Jass know…

In 2020, the COVID-19 pandemic brought a silent stillness to Bangkok's streets, a stark contrast to their usual bustling life. Yet, amid this quiet, a new pulse began to beat through the city. It was here that Arthit, a celebrated Thai actor known for his captivating screen presence, found himself putting on the green uniform of Grab, the food delivery service now becoming the city's lifeline to normalcy.

Arthit's journey began on one particular sultry afternoon. His apartment, once a temporary retreat between shoots, had become a stifling cage. He looked out at the eerily silent cityscape and decided it was time to write a new script for himself. He signed up as a Grab driver, swapping his glamorous film sets for the streets of Bangkok. On his first day, the reality of his new role settled in as he navigated the maze of the city, the green box on his scooter was a welcome sign of delicious deliveries for a pandemic depressed population.

The few customers who saw Arthit, would often do a double-take when Arthit arrived with their meals. "Aren't you...?" they would gasp through their masks, their eyes gave expressions of disbelief and excitement. But Arthit wasn't there for the fanfare. "Just a Grab driver today," he'd say with a warm, disarming smile, leaving the food at the doorstep as he turned away. His deliveries became more than transactions; they were moments of connection, shared experiences of a city holding its breath, waiting for the storm to pass.

Meanwhile, across Bangkok, the city's culinary scene was quietly reinventing itself. In the historic district, Mrs. Somchai transformed her beloved noodle shop into a bustling online kitchen. Her signature broth, once savored at colorful plastic street-side tables, was now packaged carefully for delivery. Through Grab, her flavors continued to reach the heart of Bangkok, comforting souls in a time of uncertainty.

The stories multiplied – a laid-off airline pilot, a university student saving for her tuition, a mother supporting her family. Their paths converged in this new reality, each green-liveried scooter-box a thread in Bangkok's tapestry of ingenuity. They weren't just delivering food; they were delivering fragments of hope, reminders that the city's heart still beat strong, even in the most uncertain and disconnected times.

Daily, as dusk bled into the night, Arthit's world became a canvas of shadows and streetlights, painting a picture of a city at rest yet restless. The once crowded night markets, now ghostly in their silence, whispered tales of a life paused. His journey each evening was a solitary voyage through the heart of a city holding its breath, each delivery a quiet ritual of offerings to ordinary people in the midst of isolation.

Through the empty streets, night after night, he glided, a lone figure against the backdrop of shuttered shops and dimly lit windows. The air, thick with the heat of the Thai summer, carried the faint memories of jasmine and street food, a lingering specter of days now distant. Each stop along his route was a glimpse into the lives unfolding behind closed doors - families huddled around dining tables, individuals seeking solace in the small joys of a meal shared in quietude.

The solitude of the night rides gave Arthit time to reflect. He pondered the fragility of the world he once knew, the ephemeral nature of fame and fortune. The streets of Bangkok, with their hidden corners and silent stories, became his confidants, listening to the unspoken fears and hopes of a man rediscovering himself amidst a world in turmoil.

In the quiet moments between deliveries, he found an unexpected kinship with the night – its stillness a balm to his weary soul, its stillness a companion in his journey of introspection. Bangkok, under the veil of night, was a city of contrasts – of silence and whispers, of shadows and light – and Arthit, in his green jacket, became a part of the city itself, weaving his story into its enduring narrative.

The pandemic, with its trials and tribulations, had unraveled the fabric of everyday life, but in its wake, it wove new patterns of human connection. And as the first light of dawn crept over the horizon each morning, Arthit's night would end, leaving behind the streets that had become his sanctuary, returning to a world forever changed, yet undefeated.

During the pandemic, food culture in Thailand contrasted significantly with that in the United States, particularly due to the common practice in Thai households of multiple generations living under one roof. This familial structure necessitated heightened precautions to protect the elderly, who were more vulnerable to COVID-19.

As a result, rituals like thorough decontamination for those returning from outside and the use of a serving spoon became integral to family meals. The serving spoon, in particular, emerged as a critical tool for preventing cross-contamination during shared meals.

In the U.S., where households are more often nuclear and multi-generational living is less common, these specific practices were less prevalent. Instead, American households adapted in other ways, such as increased reliance on pre-packaged foods or individual servings to minimize contact.

In both Thailand and the U.S. among other countries, food delivery services saw a significant increase in usage. In Thailand, these services became especially crucial for individuals living alone or for those unable to cook, ensuring access to prepared meals while minimizing exposure risks. The role of food delivery services in maintaining a semblance of normalcy and ensuring food security during the pandemic was invaluable across different cultures and living arrangements.

Shadows by the River

(A Short Play)

Act 1, Scene 1: "Amidst the Rubble:

Set in a small distant suburb of post-bomb Hiroshima, the scene opens with the grandmother, Eiko, and her grandson, Hiro, salvaging what they can from their devastated garden. They talk about the tragedy, their lost family, and their uncertain future. Eiko is headstrong and hopeful but weary; Hiro is determined but scared.

(The stage is set to represent a damaged garden behind a traditional Japanese house. Burnt plants, debris, and a faint outline of what was once a thriving garden are visible. Eiko, an elderly woman, is carefully tending to a surviving plant. Hiro, a teenager, is rummaging through the debris. The mood is somber, reflective.)

EIKO: (gently touching a plant) Every little leaf... a memory of what it was like here, before...

HIRO: (frustrated) I can't find anything useful, Obaachan. Everything's gone.

EIKO: (with a calm resolve) Not everything, Hiro. We still have each other, and a strong hope to rebuild.

HIRO: (looking around) But why? Why did this have to happen?

EIKO: (sighing deeply) War doesn't provide reasons. It just takes.

(Pause as both reflect on the devastation. Hiro finds a partly burnt but salvageable vegetable.)

HIRO: Look, Obaachan! This survived.

EIKO: (smiling faintly) Just like us. Maybe we can sell some. People must be hungry.

HIRO: (nods) Yes, let's go to the river market. We can't give up.

(They start to collect whatever produce they can find.)

EIKO: (pauses and looks into the distance) I remember when this garden was full of life, laughter...

HIRO: (determined) We'll bring it back to life, Obaachan. We're not defeated yet.

(They continue their work in silence, the scene conveying a mix of sorrow and hope.)

EIKO: (resolutely) Our garden will bloom again, Hiro. It must.

(Lights dim as they prepare to leave for the river, symbolizing the end of the scene and the beginning of their new journey.)

(End of Scene)

Act 1, Scene 2: "At the River Market"

At the river, people including Eiko and Hiro gather to sell and buy produce and other goods. There's a sense of community among the survivors, but also an undercurrent of despair. They're unaware of the river's contamination. Hiro interacts with other sellers, learning their stories.

(The stage transforms to depict a bustling river market scene. Various makeshift stalls are set up, with people selling and buying produce. Everyone is washing their vegetables in the water of the river. The atmosphere is a blend of desperation and community spirit. Eiko and Hiro enter with their salvaged vegetables, setting up a small stall.)

EIKO: (arranging the vegetables) Remember, Hiro, smile. It invites trust.

HIRO: (nervously) I just hope they buy something.

(A neighbor, Kenji, approaches their stall.)

KENJI: (picking up a vegetable) These look good, Eiko-san. How's your garden?

EIKO: (with a faint smile) What's left of it helps us get by.

HIRO: (interjecting) It's tough, but we're managing.

(A customer, Yumi, a young mother, approaches.)

YUMI: (eyeing the vegetables) Are these safe? I heard rumors about the river water...

EIKO: (reassuringly) We've washed them well, dear. Safety first, always.

(Yumi buys some vegetables. More people browse and buy. Hiro interacts with another young vendor, Masa.)

HIRO: (to Masa) How's business?

MASA: (shrugging) Slow. People are scared, I guess.

HIRO: (sighing) Yeah. Who wouldn't be?

(Eiko watches the crowd, her expression a mix of hope and worry.)

EIKO: (to herself) So many lives changed…

(A passerby coughs violently in the background, drawing worried glances.)

HIRO: (noticing the passerby) Obaachan, do you think…?

EIKO: (shaking her head) Let's not jump to conclusions. We need to stay strong.

(The scene closes with Eiko and Hiro continuing to sell, amidst the mixed emotions of hope, fear, and uncertainty that pervade the market.)

(End of Scene)

Act 2, Scene 1: "The Fading Light"

Eiko's health deteriorates. Hiro starts noticing others falling ill too. Conversations at the market shift from survival to the strange sickness spreading among them. Hiro grapples with the fear of losing his grandmother and the guilt of selling possibly contaminated food.

(The stage shows a small room in Eiko and Hiro's home. Eiko is lying in bed, looking frail and weak. Hiro sits beside her, a bowl of vegetable soup on a small table. The mood is somber.)

EIKO: (coughing) Hiro, the garden… have you watered the plants?

HIRO: (forcing a smile) I have, Obaachan. Don't worry about the garden.

EIKO: (weakly) Good… good. People need the food.

(A moment of silence. Hiro looks at Eiko with deep concern.)

HIRO: Obaachan, you need to eat something. Here, try some soup.

(Eiko feebly attempts to eat, then sets the spoon down.)

EIKO: Hiro, I've seen others at the market… getting sick like me.

HIROSHI: (anxiously) It's just a cold, Obaachan. You'll get better soon.

(Eiko looks at Hiro, her eyes reflecting a mix of love and sadness.)

EIKO: Hiro, you've grown so much… You're strong, kind…I wish…I wish I could stay…

HIRO: (tearfully) Obaachan, don't talk like that. You're going to be okay.

(Eiko gently holds Hiro's hand.)

EIKO: You remind me so much of your father… He would be proud of you.

(There's a knock at the door. Masa enters with a small basket of vegetables.)

MASA: (quietly) I brought some vegetables from the market.

HIRO: (nodding) Thank you, Masa.

(Masa sets down the basket, glancing worriedly at Eiko.)

MASA: (softly) Everyone's talking about the river… the water…

HIRO: (in denial) It's just rumors.

(Eiko coughs again, weaker this time. The room grows still, the gravity of the situation hanging in the air.)

EIKO: (whispering) Take care of each other… Help each other…

(Eiko's hand slowly slips from Hiro's grip. Her breathing becomes shallow. Hiro and Masa stand by, helpless and grief-stricken.)

HIRO: (whispering) Obaachan…

(The stage lights dim, leaving the room in a soft glow, symbolizing Eiko's fading presence.)

(End of Scene)

Act 2, Scene 2: "The Last Petal Falls"

Eiko, on her deathbed, reflects on her life, the beauty of Hiroshima before the bombing, and her hopes for Hiro's future. She passes away, leaving Hiro alone, but stronger and more mature. The play ends with Hiro making a vow to remember the lessons of the past and rebuild a better future.

(The stage is dimly lit, symbolizing the somber mood. Hiro is sitting alone beside Eiko's empty bed, a single candle flickering in the background. The room is filled with a profound sense of loss.)

HIRO: (softly, to himself) You always said the garden was like life… growing, blooming, then… returning to the earth.

(He stands up, walking over to the small window, looking out at the night sky.)

HIRO: (reflecting) You taught me so much, Obaachan… about strength, about hope. But how do I go on without you?

(A gentle breeze enters the room, rustling the curtains. Hiro takes a deep breath, composing himself.)

HIRO: (resolutely) I'll keep the garden alive, Obaachan. For you, for us.

(He turns back to the room, looking at the few vegetables left on the table, a reminder of Eiko's love and care.)

HIRO: (picking up a vegetable) This is more than just food… it's a part of you, Obaachan, of your legacy.

(There's a gentle knock at the door. Masa enters, hesitantly.)

MASA: Hiro, I heard about Eiko-san. I'm so sorry.

HIRO: (nodding) Thank you, Masa. She was… she was everything.

(Masa steps forward, offering a supportive presence.)

MASA: The market… everyone's talking about the river now. They're scared.

HIRO: (determined) Then we need to help them, we need to discover the truth and tell them… like Obaachan would have wanted.

(The two stand in silence, united in their resolve to move forward. Hiro's eyes are filled with a mixture of sorrow and determination as he looks out into the audience.)

HIRO: (firmly) We can't let fear take over. We have to be strong, for her, for everyone.

(The stage lights begin to fade, leaving Hiro and Masa standing together, symbolizing the beginning of a new chapter, one of rebuilding and hope in the face of a damaged environment and broken spirits.)

(End of Scene)

The atomic bombings of Hiroshima on August 6, 1945, and Nagasaki on August 9, 1945, stand as monumental events in the annals of warfare, marking the first and only instances of nuclear weapons used in armed conflict. These bombings resulted in unprecedented destruction, instantly killing tens of thousands and causing massive infrastructural damage. In Hiroshima, it is estimated that around 140,000 people died by the end of 1945, while Nagasaki saw approximately 74,000 deaths due to the bomb and its immediate aftermath.

The survivors, known as "Hibakusha," faced dire long-term health repercussions. Radiation exposure led to a significant increase in cancer rates, particularly leukemia, which showed a marked increase among those exposed to the radiation within a few years after the exposure. Other cancers, such as breast, lung, and thyroid cancer, also showed higher incidence rates in the populations of Hiroshima and Nagasaki, studies showing these effects continuing across subsequent decades.

The environmental consequences of the bombings were extremely severe. The intense heat and radiation led to significant soil and water contamination. Radioactive isotopes released by the bombs permeated the ecosystems, leading to long-term ecological disturbances. This contamination affected agriculture, with immediate effects such as black rain—a fallout-induced phenomenon causing polluted, black-colored rain to fall after the explosions—ruining crops and rendering vast tracts of agricultural land unusable for extended periods.

The lasting repercussions of the Hiroshima and Nagasaki bombings have been a subject of extensive study and reflection, highlighting the severe consequences of nuclear warfare. These events not only reshaped Japan but also had a profound impact on international relations and nuclear policy, serving as a somber reminder of the destructive capacity of nuclear weapons and shaping global disarmament efforts to ensure such a tragedy is never repeated.

When Language Fails

In the supermarket sushi stalls of Phoenix, Arizona, the finely crafted roll makers are usually from Burma, not Japan. Ask them, and they will tell you so. They are from Burma, they insist, not Japan, and rarely Myanmar…

One spring evening during an adult English class, held in one of downtown Phoenix's mega-churches, Teacher Gary paused the class's informal chat session with his trademark, "Shhh, shhh, shhh, shhh, shhh." This sound instantly brought silence as everyone in the class had been trained to Pavlovian perfection by Gary's Shhhs. Gary would now address his diverse group of students (people from over ten different countries) and their tutors, whom he called Encouragers.

Teacher Gary posed a reflective question about the purpose of their gathering, drawing everyone's attention. "Why are you here? Why do we meet here week after week?" After a short silence, he began to share an experience that had recently happened to his wife, a story that promised to add a new layer of purpose to their collective learning experience.

"Last week," Teacher Gary began, "my wife was shopping at Fry's Grocery Store. She was in a rush when she heard someone calling, 'Hey, hi.' Not recognizing the voice, she kept going forward. Then she heard the same voice calling her name. She turned and saw Pah, one of our former students, a refugee from Burma. My wife felt bad for not stopping earlier. She gave Pah a big hug, happy to see one of her old students.

"Pah was wearing a chef or bakery uniform. 'Do you work here?' my wife asked. Pah pointed to the sushi stall near the grocery store's deli section and said, 'Do you see that store over there?'"

In the classroom, about 15 students and their Encouragers, were drawn into the story, happy to hear about a former student's employment. Teacher Gary looked around the room. Silence hung in the air. Finally, with his head held high, he quoted Pah's triumphant words, "I *own* that store."

There was an audible inhale from several students, and even a joyful giggle from a few Encouragers. Gary continued, "That…that is why we are all here. The American Dream. Pah and her husband came from Burma as refugees. They didn't know English, but they came to class. They were good students and they learned.

"They worked hard, and saved money, and they learned enough English to get a business loan. Pah's husband was able to quit his job, and now they are successful business owners."

Pah told Gary's wife that she had to take some sushi home, free of charge, and that she was always welcome to come get fresh sushi from their stall in Fry's. This chance meeting was a blessing of good news and Gary was overjoyed to be able to share it with the students and Encouragers.

By now, everyone in the class had fallen silent again. One young man, Roon, leaned closer in to hear the end of the story, a slight smirk on his face. Roon was also from Burma, so this story was of particular interest to him. Gary finished the lesson by reminding the students and Encouragers that even if they feel frustrated and that they are not making progress, they are. The progress may be slow, but the goal is attainable. Everyone left feeling happier than when they came to class that night.

The very next night, the students and Encouragers were sitting in pairs, practicing English when in walked Roon, about 10 minutes late, as always, and as always, dressed to the nines, hair perfectly spiked, sporting a full forearm tattoo. But unlike always, he was carrying a huge tray of freshly made sushi which he promptly handed to Teacher Gary as a thank you gift for being such a good teacher.

Gary was flattered, and blushing. "Roon, did you make this?" Roon looked shy but proud as he said, "Yes! I made this one." Gary told Roon thank you and that he wanted to share the sushi with the class. The sushi was put in the church kitchen, and class carried on as usual with the students and Encouragers moving to the computer lab to work on Rosetta Stone together.

Suddenly everyone heard, "Shhh, shhh, shhh." What was going on? Gary never shhhed during the Rosetta Stone hour. "Everybody, everybody, please stop where you are. Just stop for a few minutes." Gary stood in the middle of the computer lab, all eyes on him. He was visibly shaken as he started to speak, "You know, we talk in this class about refugees. Many of you are refugees, but we don't often think about what that means."

Jass, one of the most experienced and intuitive Encouragers looked over to Roon's desk. It sat empty. "Shit." Jass cringed at herself for letting out a curse word in a church, but she couldn't help it. She knew Gary had very bad news and that it was about Roon.

Gary went on, "You all come here every night, we work on English together, but some of us don't realize, or don't think about, many of your families are still back home. Still in danger. Well, Roon just got a call from his wife. As some of you know, Roon is from Burma, some say Myanmar, but in Burma, when the government doesn't like you, well…they try to kill you."

The students and Encouragers were held by silence for the second night in a row. Jass looked at Xavier, her favorite student from Ecuador. His eyes were full of sorrowful knowing.

Gary continued, "Roon just got a call from his wife, and she told him that her father's house has been bombed. Now, his wife and father-in-law survived, but three people died."

Gary stopped talking for a few seconds. He couldn't find the words he needed to go on. The students and Encouragers looked at each other, sadness and understanding in their eyes. At last, Gary spoke again: "So tonight, please, remember Roon and his family in your prayers, and know…just that I am happy you are all here, that you're safe…I don't know what to say…and, um, please go back to your computers and work until 8:30."

Xavier and Jass turned back to the computer screen. A heavy silence fell between them. Jass looked to Xavier for guidance as he was older and had more life experience than she. Xavier suggested, "Let's be finished." Jass agreed. Nobody felt like working on Rosetta Stone anymore.

The two spent a few more seconds in silence before striking up a conversation about Xavier, his family, and his reasons for leaving Ecuador. It was a somber yet intimate conversation that bonded them further, not as just student/Encourager, but as two people at a loss for words save for the prayers in their hearts.

At 8:30, class officially ended. Everyone left the computer lab under hushed murmurs and stoic glances. Jass passed by the kitchen on her way out and saw Roon's sushi sitting on the counter. She wondered if it would get eaten that night, or if perhaps Teacher Gary wouldn't have the stomach for it after what had just happened.

The conflict in Burma, also known as Myanmar, has deep historical roots, extending back to the post-colonial period following World War II. This period marked the beginning of a series of complex ethnic and political tensions, particularly between the Burmese military (Tatmadaw) and various ethnic minority groups.

These conflicts have been compounded by struggles for autonomy and recognition, along with disputes over natural resources in ethnically rich areas. The military's persistent dominance in national politics has exacerbated these tensions, leading to repeated instances of severe human rights violations and extensive military crackdowns.

The ongoing strife has precipitated significant humanitarian crises, resulting in the displacement of hundreds of thousands of people. Displaced individuals have been forced to flee their homes due to violence, persecution, and the destruction of villages, often finding temporary refuge in internally displaced persons (IDP) camps within Myanmar or crossing borders into neighboring countries like Thailand, Bangladesh, and Malaysia. These refugee camps, while offering safety from immediate physical danger, frequently struggle with inadequate resources to properly support the growing numbers of refugees.

A significant number of these displaced individuals have also sought and found refuge in the United States. The journey to the U.S. and the subsequent resettlement process pose distinct challenges, including cultural adaptation and navigating a complex immigration bureaucracy. Despite these obstacles, the Burmese refugee population has striven to integrate into American society.

Their efforts to preserve their rich cultural identities—through language, cuisine, religious practices, and community organizations—have enriched the multicultural landscape of the U.S. Moreover, many refugees have become active contributors to their local economies and communities, enhancing social diversity and fostering cross-cultural understanding.

In essence, while the conflict in Myanmar has led to significant suffering and displacement, it has also given rise to stories of resilience and positive contribution as displaced individuals build new lives in the U.S., adding to the country's cultural mosaic and underscoring the complex interplay between migration, identity, and integration.

A significant number of Burmese refugees have resettled in Arizona, integrating into various aspects of local life and economy. Many of these refugees have found employment in the food industry, particularly in sushi shops located inside grocery stores. Some have even taken the entrepreneurial step of owning these establishments.

The Most Holy Trinity

Fareed, a community college student in the United States, carried not just the weight of his academic ambitions but also the heavy memories of his life in Somalia. As a refugee, his journey was marked by loss and courage. In Somalia, Fareed was immersed in political studies, navigating the complexities of a country rife with conflict.

In the United States, Fareed found solace in the kitchen of a Somali restaurant, where he worked. Here, he reconnected with his roots through his mother's recipe for sambusa. Fareed's days were split between the steamy kitchen, where the aroma of sambusa filled the air, and the halls of the community college, where he strived to master English.

The language lessons, often challenging, were made smoother by the presence of his tutors and peers, who were regularly treated to Fareed's delicious sambusa. Each pastry, filled with savory meat and spices, was not just a snack but a narrative of a culture, a family, and a journey across continents. Fareed walked with a particular bounce in his step on days he brought the sambusa to share with everyone.

Jass grew to recognize this step, and knew what deliciousness lay ahead even before she saw the oil-stained paper bag

full of pastries swinging in Fareed's
hand.

During one particular tutoring session,
Fareed, usually reticent about his past,
opened up to Jass, his favorite tutor. An
English teacher gave the assignment:
Write about your worst memory. In
Jass's opinion, this was a bad choice for
a writing assignment in a class full of
refugees, but Fareed needed to finish the
paper nonetheless. He chose to recount
the day he lost his father. He narrated
the story with a stoic calmness born of
too much seen too young.

The most harrowing day of his life came
with the sound of gunshots – the day Al
Shabaab militants took his father's life.
He heard distant gunshots and then saw
his mother running towards their house.
His mother's return home, her tears
mingling with words of grief, painted a

memory Fareed would carry with him always. His mother collapsed telling her sons their father had just been shot.

Fareed didn't cry while recounting this story, and Jass helped him get his words on paper. After the assignment was finished, the topic turned to Al Shabaab, and how crazy they were. Fareed chuckled when he explained to Jass how Al Shabaab had actually outlawed sambusa because they were triangle shaped, with three sides, and this was way too close of a resemblance to the Christian Holy Trinity of the Father, Son, and Holy Spirit.

The group, Al Shabaab, which adheres to a strict interpretation of Sharia law, imposed numerous restrictions on daily life within the territories it controls. The ban on sambusas was part of a broader set of prohibitions that included banning music, movies, and various cultural and sporting activities that the group deems un-Islamic.

Jass listened, the tragedy of Fareed's story lending a new gravity to the sambusa they often enjoyed. The freedom to cook his mother's sambusa was a simple yet profound blessing, and from that day on, Jass appreciated those delicious stuffed pastries more than anyone could know.

*****

The conflict in Somalia, significantly shaped by the militant group Al-Shabaab, has been a key factor in the displacement of many Somalis, leading to a large refugee population, including those who have resettled in the United States. There are currently between 30,000 and 150,000 Somalis living in the US.

Al-Shabaab, emerging around 2006, originally functioned as a militia affiliated with the Islamic Courts Union (ICU) before evolving into a more independent and extreme entity. Their actions have included insurgency against Somalia's Transitional Federal Government, affiliations with al-Qaeda, and implementation of a strict interpretation of Islamic law often at odds with local Somali practices.

Al-Shabaab's rise significantly contributed to the instability and violence in Somalia, including targeted attacks against civilians and government forces. This environment of conflict and insecurity has led to widespread displacement within Somalia and beyond its borders. As a result, many Somalis have sought refuge in other countries, including the United States, where they have sought to rebuild their lives and contribute to their new communities.

In the U.S., Somali refugees face various challenges, including adapting to a new culture and environment. Despite these hurdles, they often find ways to connect with their heritage, such as through culinary ventures. This connection is evident in the emergence of Somali restaurants and food businesses, which serve as cultural hubs and provide employment opportunities for the refugee community.

The situation in Somalia remains complex and challenging, with ongoing conflict and humanitarian crises. The adaptability of the Somali people, both within their country and as part of diaspora communities, highlight their enduring spirit in the face of adversity.

The Fragile Husk

In the shadowed embrace of the New Mexico desert, a stretch of highway holds a solemn vigil. Here, a mother constructs her shrine, a roadside memorial for her son, whose life was stolen by the swift cruelty of fate. This memorial, nestled against the backdrop of the relentless sagebrush and caliche, becomes her sanctuary, a place where plastic flowers fade in the sun, and the corn husks of a loved dish dry out and blow away, moving down the highway and into the arroyo like ghosts.

The mother always brings with her tamales, his favorite dish, each one lovingly wrapped in corn husks – a culinary tradition passed down through generations, now a bitter-sweet symbol of her loss. The tamales, filled with spiced meat and steamed to tender perfection, are more than mere food; they are vessels of memories, echoes of laughter that once filled her home.

As the days pass, the unforgiving sun beats down upon the shrine, the tamales begin their inevitable surrender to decay. They sit, a humble offering to the merciless environment, their once steaming warmth giving way to the chill of the night. The transformation is stark – a once comforting meal now sacrifice to the harsh reality of impermanence.

The desert night descends, and with it, a haunting quietude. The tamales, under the silver-blue moonlight, become spectral figures in this mournful tableau. They are like her son's abandoned dreams, their gradual decay mirroring the erosion of her own hopes for his future. Fragile husks blowing away. Always like ghosts.

In this desolate space, where the boundary between the living and the dead seems to blur, she feels his presence. The husks, now part of the landscape, become a bridge to the world he now inhabits, a world beyond her reach, yet one she touches through this act of remembrance. Husks. A mother's embrace. A son, giving up the ghost.

The memorial stands, with its faded cross, its faded pictures, its burned out candles. These are placed as silent sentinels to a mother's enduring love, a mother's tribute to the son she lost, a testament to the unyielding bond that not even death can sever.

In the heart of the sagebrush, rocks, and valleys, by the roadside, this mother seeks a solemn peace, a space to hold her son in her heart, as enduring and vast as the New Mexico sky.

*****

Roadside memorials in the Southwest United States have a deep-rooted history, serving as stark reminders of the lives lost in motor vehicle accidents. These memorials often include personalized elements such as the deceased's name, significant dates, inspirational quotes, and even small trinkets that reflect the personality of the loved one.

While some families choose to create homemade memorials, others may opt for government-provided signs that include cautionary messages for motorists. These memorials are not only a way to honor the deceased but also act as a visual reminder to drivers about the importance of safety on the roads.

The practice, deeply embedded in the culture of the American Southwest, speaks to the personal and public nature of grief and remembrance.

It's not uncommon for people to leave food at roadside memorials, although this practice varies based on cultural traditions and personal preferences. In some cultures, leaving food is a way to honor the deceased and is seen as a symbolic offering.

Prayer Bread

It's 7:00am in Amarillo, Texas. An alarm is sounding, its shrillness cutting through the air. Glenda, head baker of Kind House Ukraine Bakery, shuffles to her industrial-sized oven to take out loaves of prayer bread. It's also 3:00pm in Dnipro, Ukraine, and a different kind of alarm is sounding, an air-raid siren. People shuffle to any kind of shelter that they can find.

The prayer bread, bread Glenda and her volunteers had kneaded that morning, imbuing the dough with blessings and wishes for the safety of thousands of people, both loved ones and strangers living halfway around the world, was hot and ready to be sold. In Dnipro, Amarillo's sister city, people are unaware of the prayer bread being baked in their name, yet they are not wholly unaffected by the activities of the bakery…

It had been more than ten years since Glenda had fallen in love with the people of Ukraine. She visited them as much as she could, volunteering, teaching, learning, and loving. During the annexation of Crimea, Glenda was at a loss about what to do. How could she help? She went to her mother for advice. Her mom looked her in the eyes and made one simple yet profound statement: "You're gonna learn to bake."

Empowered by her mother's advice, Glenda embraced the cinnamon roll recipe handed down in her family for generations. She began baking these treats, turning each swirl of dough and sprinkle of cinnamon into an act of charity. People, drawn by the scent of freshly baked goods and the spirit of the cause, would donate money in exchange for the rolls.

Glenda's front porch was slowly transformed into a community hub, a makeshift storefront where assorted baked goods awaited hungry and compassionate visitors. Generosity flourished as patrons not only paid for what they took but also left behind flour, sugar, and other baking essentials, fueling Glenda's mission.

Over the years, the funds raised from these humble beginnings grew into a substantial force for good. Glenda channeled this generosity into aiding those affected by the Crimea conflict, and extending support to Ukrainian orphanages and schools. Her small, heartfelt initiative blossomed into a beacon of hope and solidarity, touching countless lives beyond her own community.

As the crisis in Ukraine escalated with the Russian invasion, Glenda recognized that her front porch bakery was no longer sufficient for the growing needs. In response, she established the Kind House Ukraine Bakery (KHUB) as an official storefront in the middle of town where people could come make their delicious selections. The bakery became a hub of community support and solidarity.

People from all walks of life poured in to volunteer, donate items, and buy baked goods, contributing whatever they felt was appropriate. Funds collected were directed towards supporting those affected in Ukraine, providing essential supplies and assistance for evacuation efforts. KHUB embodied the spirit of community-driven support, turning every purchase and donation into tangible aid for those in need.

So many mornings at the bakery started the same way: As the shrillness of Glenda's morning oven alarm fades into the bustling sounds of her bakery, distant sirens in Dnipro signal a starkly different mood for the day.

Amid these contrasting worlds, the loaves of prayer bread emerge from the oven, golden, fragrant and ready to be packaged and purchased by donations from the good people of Amarillo, Texas.

Unbeknownst to many seeking shelter in Dnipro and other Ukrainian cities, each loaf of bread and baked good from Amarillo carries unseen blessings and a silent message of solidarity.

Kind House Ukraine Bakery has helped hundreds of orphans and heated 170 homes from 2018 to 2022. They also rescued 2,000 people out of the harshest areas of Ukraine and brought them to safety in 2022. In 2023, they built a kitchen that feeds over 400 children and hundreds of adults weekly (kindhousebakery.org).

The organization, led by the saintly Glenda, continues to bake and send proceeds to people in Ukraine, and as of this writing, in 2024, Russia continues its full-scale invasion of the sovereign country of Ukraine.

Prashada, Ji

While playing the epic computer game *Sid Meier's Civilization VI*, you can choose to found a religion, Sikhism, and you can choose the ability of "Feed the World." This ability highlights the importance of nourishment, equality, and community—all concepts that have always resonated with me personally...

When I was young, I often accompanied my mom to deliver Meals-on-Wheels. I'm not sure if my passion for volunteer work started then or earlier, but these experiences definitely reinforced the importance of sharing food and fostering human connections.

Each morning, mom and I would pull up to the industrial kitchen to collect our daily meal load along with the correct number of small cardboard milk cartons and a daily selection of fresh fruit. The meals resembled those from a hospital or elementary school, with selections including enchiladas with beans, Salisbury steak with mashed potatoes, or lasagna with salad and a brownie.

The food didn't seem very appetizing, but it was never really about the food. It was during these visits to older, homebound individuals that I truly developed my love for feeding people. After our little old minivan was fully loaded, we would start visiting houses, going down our checklist for the day.

Some people had dietary restrictions, while others simply accepted every part of the meal with a smile. They often offered my mom and me their brownie, cookie, or milk, both as a thank you and as a gracious way to refuse part of the meal they didn't want.

But one thing they always wanted was to sit and talk. Delivering the meals generally involved a short visit, which was always shorter than the clients would have liked. Often, the meal delivery from my mom and me would be the only human interaction these individuals had for weeks, or even months. They treasured these visits, and while I took it for granted at the time, I now realize I was receiving many treasures myself.

I wasn't a Sikh then, but when I found Sikhi, my love for preparing and sharing food as an act of making connections simmered into place like the final, perfect spice in a divine recipe.

After I first heard about Sikhi, I hungered for more knowledge. I traveled to Amritsar three times to study Punjabi and Sikh history in the land of the Gurus. Each visit deepened my understanding and appreciation for the practices that form the core of this vibrant faith. As I immersed myself in the culture, I also experienced firsthand the pivotal role of the Langar (community meals) in Sikh community life.

Food was plentiful in Amritsar, and the Langar halls were always bustling yet welcoming spaces. In these halls, people would come and go all day, every day, enjoying a meal or snack before entering the Gurudwara. In the U.S., it was customary for people to partake in a Langar meal after attending a large Gurudwara gathering. This twist on the Langar tradition was inspired by people in the U.S. eating together after a church services. For the same reason, many large Sikh gatherings take place on Sundays in the U.S.

In contrast, in Punjab, the original tradition typically involved eating before entering the religious space to avoid distractions caused by hunger. Likewise, Gurudwaras in Punjab are open twenty-four hours a day, seven days per week, and year-round. You can find people worshiping there around the clock.

Also, in Punjab, one could eat before, after, or at any time during a Sikh celebration because Sikhs are committed to feeding people of all religions. Nobody was required to visit the inside of the Gurudwara or partake in Gurudwara activities to receive a meal, though many chose to do so, drawn by the inviting and peaceful atmosphere.

My favorite Langar hall was at the Baba Deep Singh Gurudwara. Although it wasn't the largest in the area, it was where I felt most at ease. I met my friend via Facebook, Gursevek there several times, and we would sit side by side sipping chai as sevadars occasionally passed by, offering "Prashada, Ji?"

In the traditional manner of Langar halls, Sikhs and others sat together on the floor, extending both hands upwards to receive the flat, round roti bread. Accepting the bread with both hands is a gesture of reverence, symbolizing the honor of receiving a gift from God, the prashad, a sacred offering.

Langar doesn't necessarily have to take place inside a Langar hall. One surprising and delightful experience was the drive-by Langar that happened on holidays or whenever sevadars felt moved to offer it. One day, while Auntie, Uncle, and I were on our way to the market, Uncle suddenly, and without any apparent reason, pulled our little white sedan over to the side of the road and rolled down all of our windows.

Three Sikhs approached and offered each of us a large bowl made of leaves filled with sabzi and a sweet square of burfi nestled on a napkin. After exchanging greetings and thanks, we continued on our way, enjoying our Langar meal in the car.

The more I was nourished in Punjab, the more I reminisced about my volunteer work with my mom and my penchant for feeding others. Then, as now, it wasn't just about the food—it was about community, connection, and for Sikhs, it also embraced principles of equality and a reverence for God's abundance and the gift of nourishment. It was during this period that I decided to take a stab at the role of sevadar in the largest Langar hall in the world.

Gursevek was a sevadar in the Langar hall of Darbar Sahib, also known as the Golden Temple. One afternoon, I asked him to show me around the kitchen, and he eagerly led me up several sets of stairs above the eating area to a few large concrete rooms and hidden red brick halls. There, men and women joyfully toiled, making roti by hand, even though roti machines were available.

As we walked outside of the bustling kitchen, Gursevek pointed out some pockmarked red bricks in the walls of an upstairs platform. He explained that these were bullet holes from Operation Blue Star in 1984, when the Indian Army entered the temple complex and opened fire on many of people inside.

The operation led to significant damage and casualties, and the marks were a somber reminder of the temple's turbulent history. Looking at the bullet holes, and then looking back into the kitchen at all of the sevadars, the importance of nourishment and Guru Nanak's vision of community meals amidst scars of violence was strikingly evident. It was now my turn to be a part of this rich tradition.

After the little tour of the broken architecture and the kitchen areas, together, Gursevek and I gathered stacks of roti and descended to the first-level Langar hall.

I was nervous, but Gursevek just smiled at me and started walking down the row of seated people, repeating the familiar "Prashada, Ji."

In Gurudwaras, anyone can perform any seva they wish; no special experience is required, nor are there forms to fill out. You simply dive in and do your best to meet the needs. Thus, I walked up and down each row, shyly repeating, "Prashada, Ji," placing a warm flatbread into the open hands of those who desired it.

Some people bowed their heads in acceptance, while others looked up at me and nodded their heads in appreciation. Some uttered words of gratitude as well. Everyone was kind, and I was humbled to be offering this bread to people, their ready hands awaiting God's gift.

It was an experience I will never forget, forever etched in my heart as the day I truly understood the profound joy of selfless service and the continued connections made by sharing food with others.

*****

Historically, Sikhs have been renowned for their commitment to feeding as many people as possible, dating back to the founding of the religion. Indeed, some Sikh places of worship provide meals for up to 100,000 people each day!

The tradition of Langar, a communal kitchen and free meal service, is a central aspect of Sikhism, embodying the religion's principles of selfless service and equality. The concept was initiated by Guru Nanak, the founder of Sikhism, in the early 16th century. He started this practice to emphasize the equality of all people regardless of religion, caste, color, creed, age, gender, or social status—a revolutionary idea at the time.

The practice was institutionalized by the third Sikh Guru, Guru Amar Das, who established Langar as a mandatory practice in all Sikh Gurudwaras. This served multiple purposes: it ensured that all who came to seek the Guru's wisdom would not leave hungry, it reinforced the principle of equality by having everyone sit on the floor together to eat the same food, and it provided a practical demonstration of the Sikh principles of sharing and selfless service (Seva).

Langar is typically vegetarian to accommodate the dietary restrictions of any person who may visit the Gurudwara. The food is prepared by volunteers who engage in this service as a form of devotion. Volunteers also serve the meals and clean up afterwards, reflecting the community-oriented and egalitarian spirit of Sikhism.

Over the centuries, the tradition of Langar has continued and expanded globally with Sikh communities worldwide. In many places, it has adapted to include support during disasters, feeding protestors or the homeless, and other acts of community service, always free of charge and open to all, truly embodying Guru Nanak's vision of a world without social, religious, or economic divisions.

Breaking Bread, Opening Hearts

In the chilly embrace of a late September evening, Ethan wandered into the expansive field that served as the stage for the Bread and Puppet Theater. With only a thin jacket to shield him from the crisp Vermont air, he felt the first stir of anticipation.

A lifelong resident of a neighboring small town, Ethan had grown up hearing tales of the theater's legendary performances but had never witnessed one himself. Tonight, propelled by curiosity and a recent stirring in his own conscience, he came alone to see their latest offering—a play about genocide.

As the sky darkened to a deep indigo, the spectacle began. The field, lit by soft, ambient lights, transformed into a vivid tableau of stark shadows and flickering figures. Towering puppets, some the height of small trees, emerged silently, their exaggerated, haunting features cutting through the night. The theme was somber, touching on the tragic history of genocides across the ages—from Armenia to Rwanda to the largest genocide in history, the Holocaust against Jewish people, and finally, the recent scars in the Middle East.

Ethan found himself absorbed by the poignant simplicity of the puppets' movements, choreographed to a melancholy tune played on a lone violin. The music wove through the audience like a thread binding them together in shared grief. Each scene depicted not just the brutality of the oppressors, but also the power and unity of those who suffered. It was a stark portrayal of humanity's darkest tendencies and its enduring strength.

At intermission, bread was passed around—homemade, dense, and slightly sweet. Eating it, Ethan felt an unexpected kinship with the strangers around him, all united under the night sky, partaking in this age-old ritual of breaking bread. The play resumed, and with each scene, Ethan felt his understanding deepen. He was no longer just a bystander; he felt a part of the narrative, woven into the fabric of the play's mournful yet resistive textile.

The final act left the audience in a powerful silence, broken only by the gentle rustling of leaves in the breeze. As the puppets retreated slowly, their shadows receding into the night, Ethan remained seated, letting the waves of emotion wash over him. The performance had ended, but the message lingered, echoing in his mind—the reminder of past atrocities, and the collective responsibility to prevent them in the future.

Walking back to his car, the bread now a comforting weight in his stomach, Ethan felt changed. The play had not only depicted the horrors of genocide but had also illuminated the continuing spirit of solidarity and survival.

He realized that while the past could not be undone, the future was still in the hands of those who remembered and

learned from it. Tonight, he was one of
them.

Bread and Puppet Theater is an iconic and influential puppet theater, known for its large-scale performances and its radical, political storytelling. Founded in 1963 by Peter Schumann on New York City's Lower East Side, the theater has long been involved in the avant-garde scene and is renowned for its experimental use of the art of puppetry to explore and critique social issues.

Peter Schumann, originally from Silesia and later moving to the U.S. from Germany, began Bread and Puppet Theater in part as a response to the Vietnam War. The theater's name derives from its early practice of serving bread to the audience as a means to create community, reflecting Schumann's vision that art is as essential as bread for human survival.

The bread, traditionally made by Schumann himself, was meant to be eaten while viewing the performances, symbolizing the union of sustenance with the food for thought provided by the puppetry.

Bread and Puppet's performances are characterized by their gigantic puppets and masks, some towering several feet high, created from simple materials like cardboard, papier-mâché, and cloth. The theater's aesthetic is rustic and deliberately rough, emphasizing the hand-made and communal aspect of the art form. Performances are typically underscored by a blend of live music, dance, and voice, creating a rich, multi-sensory experience.

The themes of Bread and Puppet's performances have consistently revolved around major social and political issues including anti-war protests, environmental conservation, and critiques of capitalism. The theater uses a very direct, poignant, and often satirical approach to storytelling which has been both celebrated and controversial.

Bread and Puppet Theater has been a significant cultural force in American and international theater, influencing countless artists and groups with its unique blend of performative protest and community engagement. The theater moved to a farm in Glover, Vermont, in 1974, which now serves as its base of operations.

The theater continues to perform both locally and around the world, maintaining its commitment to social justice and community arts. Its approach to performance as a form of political activism and communal expression remains a profound aspect of its identity and legacy.

Bread and Puppet is one of the longest-running nonprofit theaters in the U.S. and remains a vibrant part of the global arts and activism scene, sticking to its deep roots in promoting social change through creative, communal means.

Sugar Coated

One of the first students that I worked with at GateWay Community College whom I will never forget was named Aleksandra. I was 29, newly transplanted to Phoenix, and only had about four years of teaching under my belt. Aleksandra had come to GateWay to work on her English conversation skills. She was from Ukraine and had lived in the United States for about five years when I first met her.

Her English was good, and we understood each other easily. She and I both had a sweet-tooth and she, identifying me as a sweet soul sister early on, always brought little wrapped fruit Roshen candy to our tutoring sessions. We would sit and talk well past our designated half-hour appointment, candy wrappers stacking up in little piles at the corners of the desk, stories told, written down, or just spoken. But everything remembered well.

To this day, every time I start to wonder about the purpose of life and begin to spiral into one of those dismal, self-centered existential crises that we all suffer from, I think of one of the first stories that Aleksandra ever told me while working together on an ESL assignment.

She unwrapped a cherry flavored candy and started, "After the Soviet Union fell, so many people lost jobs, lost…everything. I worked at a drug company, factory, bottling pills. So many people killed themselves, so poor everybody. My husband, he just died. I don't know what to do then. One day, I just went out to walk. I felt so lost. I just walked in the street. So many people had jumped from buildings. I was just walking in the streets. I saw an old friend. She was…travel…agent? Yes, she was a travel agent, and she saw me. We talked. She told me, 'You can work for me.' I worked for her after that, and from then, I saw so many things!"

I loved this story and wanted to hear more. During our sessions, I asked her about her travels and some of her favorite memories. She talked to me about going on cruises and dancing with celebrities. With joyful, crystal blue eyes sparkling, she proclaimed, "At that time I was so young. I was beautiful and so young. I danced all night. Sometimes with actors!"

Aleksandra was now in her 70s. By my calculations, she would have been in her late 40s or 50s at that time, so it struck me as quite interesting that she said she had been "so young." It must be one of those perspectives on age that only comes much later in life. I wondered how I might see myself in my 50s looking back from my 70s. I listened on and looked more carefully at her round glowing face.

As she spoke, I could see a young girl in her eyes. Aleksandra, I'm sure, was still just as beautiful as she was in her youth if even more so now given her air of wisdom and maturity. She explained that her favorite place was the beach of the Black Sea and that on many cruises she loved seeing the beaches, but that maybe her favorite place was also Paris.

She looked contemplative every time we met, as though she constantly realized that she had lived many lifetimes in one short time, and that it was due to the happenstance of her being on the right street at the right time, meeting the right friend, and that when your world feels as though it is falling down around you in the despair of financial, familial, and societal ruin, there is the possibility of not just survival, but the birth of a whole new and beautiful life, so far removed from what you once knew that you could not even begin to imagine what magnificent experiences it might bring.

Now, here in the U.S. in 2011, she told me many times that she was so happy and thrilled that her journey had given her the opportunity to speak English with Americans in the United States. I felt humbled and always blushed when I replied, telling her that I was the one who felt blessed to learn about the world from her.

When she passed the first major grammar test in her ESL class, after studying with me for long hours, she brought me a gift of chocolate-covered pomegranate seeds. It was a major departure from our usual fruit jellies, and the significance did not escape me. I opened the bag right away and shared some with her and we started our next lesson munching chocolates. I had never before tasted anything so sweet.

This is one of the first stories I collected while working at GateWay Community College. There, I started keeping a list of students' home countries. At GateWay, I had the honor of working with, listening to, and getting to know students from over 50 countries including: Ukraine, Afghanistan, Liberia, Zimbabwe, Argentina, Korea, Australia, Brazil, Tanzania, England, Burma, Burundi, Yemen, United Arab Emirates,

Cameroon, Turkey, Iraq, Kenya, China, Syria, Sudan, Colombia, Congo (Democratic Republic), Egypt, Lebanon, Mexico, Nigeria, Eritrea, Sudan, South Sudan, Somalia, Somali Land, Ethiopia, Pakistan, the Philippines, Gambia, Congo, Senegal, India, Rwanda, Qatar, Saudi Arabia, Kosovo, Chad, Djibouti, Japan, Indonesia, and Iran.

This list seemed to grow by a few countries each semester, and with each semester, I learned a little more about the strange, beautiful, and cruel world in which we all live, all through the stories of the people who have traveled from their home countries to Europe, to Canada, to the Middle East, South America, all over the world, and finally, to Phoenix, Arizona.

*****

When the Soviet Union collapsed in 1991, Ukraine, like many former Soviet republics, faced a period of profound upheaval and transformation. This era was marked by immense challenges and significant changes that reshaped the country on multiple levels—politically, economically, and socially.

Ukraine declared its independence from the Soviet Union on August 24, 1991. The move toward independence was affirmed by a national referendum in December 1991, where over 90% of Ukrainian voters supported the decision.

The transition from a single-party system dominated by the Communist Party to a multiparty democracy was fraught with difficulties. The country struggled with the creation of a new constitution and the establishment of independent governance structures.

The economic impact of the Soviet Union's collapse on Ukraine was severe and immediate. The country faced a drastic decline in industrial output and a significant drop in GDP. The transition from a centrally planned economy to a market economy was rocky, marked by hyperinflation, a steep increase in unemployment, and widespread poverty.

Many state-owned enterprises were privatized, often in opaque processes that led to the concentration of wealth and power in the hands of a few, giving rise to the oligarch class.

Socially, the post-Soviet years were also tough. The standard of living plummeted for most of the population, healthcare systems deteriorated, and educational institutions struggled with reduced funding and outdated materials. The rapid changes and uncertainties led to a decline in public morale and an increase in emigration, as many Ukrainians sought better opportunities abroad.

Emotionally, the collapse of the Soviet Union and the subsequent changes induced a mix of hope and despair among the Ukrainian people. There was hope for political and economic freedom and a better future independent of Soviet control. However, the immediate hardships, the disruption of social services, and the instability brought about by rapid changes led to widespread despair and a sense of disorientation. Many felt disconnected from the promising future they had envisioned as the realities of corruption, economic struggle, and political chaos unfolded.

Dessert

The culinary tales captured in "On War, Food and Gods" carry us across continents, through war-torn landscapes, and into the heart of human endurance. These stories, collected from firsthand accounts and personal narratives, unveil not only the challenges faced by those in conflict zones but also their remarkable ability to find solace and resistance through their culinary heritage.

As we journeyed through each narrative, the resilience and adaptability of individuals emerged through their efforts to preserve and adapt their culinary practices under the strains of war and displacement.

This exploration reveals how, amid the turmoil of war, food transcends its role as mere sustenance. It becomes a profound element of cultural identity and a vital form of emotional and psychological support. The act of preparing a familiar dish serves as a reminder of home, a gesture of defiance against the chaos, and a hope for future peace. In places where societal structures are disrupted, the rituals of cooking and eating can offer a semblance of normalcy and a space for communal gathering and support.

Reflecting on these narratives prompts us to appreciate the deeper significance of our own food traditions and the role they play in shaping our identities. It encourages us to engage more thoughtfully with the ingredients we use, the dishes we prepare, and the cultural stories they tell. Furthermore, it inspires us to support initiatives that help protect and revive the culinary practices of communities affected by conflict, recognizing these efforts as integral to cultural preservation and recovery.

As we close this book, we are called to carry forward the spirit of unity and resilience exemplified by the individuals in these stories. We can extend the table of brotherhood by sharing these stories in our communities, advocating for policy changes that recognize the importance of cultural preservation in humanitarian aid, and supporting organizations that focus on food security and cultural identity in their relief efforts.

The global community has a role to play in ensuring that the nourishment of the body and soul, so critical in times of peace, is not forgotten in times of war. By integrating an understanding of the cultural dimensions of food into our responses to crises, we can help affected populations maintain their cultural integrity and pave the way for healing and rebuilding.

This text not only educates and informs us about the struggles faced by others—it also enriches our understanding of the power of human creativity and the unbreakable connection between food and cultural identity. Let this book serve as a reminder of our shared responsibilities and inspire us to take meaningful actions that affirm our common humanity.

Through the universal language of food, let us continue to build bridges, foster understanding, and contribute to a world where cultural diversity is celebrated and preserved, even in the face of adversity. In doing so, we honor the stories of those who have turned to their kitchens and hearths for survival, demonstrating that even in the darkest times, the human spirit finds a way to express itself and connect with others.

www.ingramcontent.com/pod-product-compliance
Lightning Source LLC
Chambersburg PA
CBHW051306250726
48656CB00004B/1495